apsara in new york

D0864636

poems

sokunthary svay

Willow Books, a Division of Aquarius Press

Detroit, Michigan

apsara in new york

Copyright © 2017 by Sokunthary Svay

All rights reserved. No part of this publication may be reproduced, stored in a retrieval system, or transmitted in any form, or by any means, electronic, mechanical, recording, photocopying or otherwise without the prior written permission of the publisher.

Editor: Randall Horton
Cover art: Chanel Matsunami Govreau

ISBN 978-0-9992232-3-9
LCCN 2017951946

Willow Books, a Division of Aquarius Press
www.WillowLit.net

Credits
The following poems have appeared, in one form or another, in the following places:

"No Radio" in *Belleville Park Pages*
"At Least Prostitutes Bring Home Money" in *Blue Lyra Review*
"Embody" in *Common Ground Review*
"No Others," "Mother Tongue," "Reincarnation" and "Don't Let Your Heritage Be Paste Tense" in *Consequence*
"Molding" and "Baptism" in *LONTAR: Journal for Southeast Asian Speculative Fiction*
"No Radio" reprinted in *The Margins*
"Mekong Song" in *Mekong Review*
"Common Ground," "Reading Between the Ribcage," "Circumference" and "Initiation" in *Newtown Literary*
"Jungle Crossing, 1980," "Dear Grandmother," "When Motherhood is Suffering" and "Daughter-in-Waiting" in *Perigee*

Printed in the United States of America

Contents

Apsara in New York

What hand framed this chalk drawing

    for fallen deities from Cambodia's kingdom?

        Flash.

      Camera turns living deities into halved beings

      below the white cloud of light and chalk.

Cotton and silk sarongs cradle cellophane-wrapped treats.

                                         Graduation.

Chalk airplane hovers above my mother and her plaid. Her eyes far away.

She's not heard of New York.

      Angkor towers crown apsara heads, different shades of olive.

The airplane ascends above Cambodia's national monument

    beyond their powdery orbs.

Dedicated to the memory of my brother, Svay Sothear, to all the Khmers lost during the Khmer Rouge era, and to my Khmer American community which still struggles with this dark legacy.

Jungle Crossing, 1980

The fields are rife with landmines.
Legs and arms rain down like Nixon's bombs
on the Cambodia-Vietnam border
bruising the ground with craters.
This is how they raped the land.

Our ancient enemy, the Vietnamese,
extend soldiers and appendages across our border
once more. In their exodus
gaunt Cambodians meet pirates
who strip their dignity for gold
as Thai refugee camps bed them
beside dirty soldiers and first world promises.

I recall the Phnom Penh of our teens
bursting with succulent juice
from pomelos ripped from their peels
spraying the boardwalk.

Remember the monsoons
when floods meant ponds   for children
good crops meant families ate   year-round
when life and living still mattered.

Music plays from an unknown distance.
Survivors gather to resume
a dance unfinished
          unfurling their fingers
                        in gestures
          once described
as lotus blossoming.

No Others

SVAY CHY AKA NGET PHENG
Ethnicity: Khmer
DPOB: Jan. 09-51, TAKEO
Occupation: Soldier/Farmer

Dependents

1. LONG YIM, F, 1956, WIFE, Occupation: Housewife/Farmer
2. *SVAY SOTHY, M, Jun-14-73, SON
3. SVAY SOKUNTHARY, F, Jul-21-80, DAUGHTER

Has very poor eyesight

List family tree and current status.

P.A.	Spouse
Svay Tuy, 62 yrs, Father, Dead	Long Sen, 48 yrs, Father, Missing
Ngeth Kun 57 yrs, Mother, Dead	Sem Heang, 48 yrs, Mother, Missing
Svay Soarn, 35 yrs, Brother, Dead	Long Sreang, 20 yrs, Brother, Missing
	Long Sry, 17 yrs, Brother, Missing
	Long Sok Han, 15 yrs, Sister, Missing
	Long Srey Kea, 13 yrs, Sister, Missing

NO OTHERS

Her American Life

She prays to her altar
says God, but means something else.

Incense hangs in the room,
ancestral spirits.

Down the elevator, Spanish speakers
pretend she can't understand "Filipina."

Khmer karaoke blares through a steel door.
Down the hallway, neighbors mistake it for Chinese.

Jehovah's Witnesses ring on weekends.
She holds her breath until voices fade.

Fearless German roaches dot the kitchen,
walls coated yellow from past deep-fried dinners.

A frozen bird defrosts under trickle of water.
Home from work, a plate of dismembered meat.

An archive of sequined and puffy sleeves
from previous decades in the closet.

Windows keep out bugs
not midnight basketball games.

She kisses her husband goodnight to separate beds
in lonesome rooms where sons once slept.

At Least Prostitutes Bring Home Money

Why you come home late in the dark
You wear the dress and stupid big boot no job

Where the money you want me save?
At least *prostitute* bring home money

What you want for dinner—noodle again?
Yeah you like your big noodle

Don't worry about freckle American men like that
Go to college get marry then work bring home money

I bring home money from hotel tip
You see my shoe only ten dollar on sale at Macy

Hey your period not come yet
Don't worry we *take care of it*

Your Daddy say he so sad you not sleep in your room
Why you go out?

Your brother visit work on his day off
He not even bring home money!

My whole life you never know who I am
I work too hard but all my children hurt me

And your daddy send his family all the money I bring home.

Portrait of a Cleaning Lady

Each morning she suits up
in a dry-cleaned navy blue uniform
her name stitched in baby blue.

She clocks in at Times Square
among a frenzy of accented workers,
polishing faucets and her English.

She wears permanent gloves
in dried, cracked lines.

The housekeeping cart
screeches, reminds her of the train
outside her housing development.

A mere 4'11"
she's mistaken for Chinese,
freckled beside aging almond eyes,
short perm and dark dye
teeth composed like a magazine smile,
belly trembling from four children.

Make Room for Tenderness

I don't want fail my kids like parents fail the black kids. Why they to listen to that music? It bad enough we have to move to the projects, where everyone think we Chinese. I'm afraid to come home late here. I have to watch my back or one of the guy rob me.

       They think they know us,

              but I know them. They all hang around with their big pants and attitude, make babies they can't take care. They should go to school or get a job. I just want make it safe to raise my kids. I don't want my kids have the same problem. I not protect their brother who die, so maybe if they not listen to rap or like the lifestyle, I see them live longer, see them succeed.

The Khmer Speaks through Palms

Sompeah
> is when palms unite
> in a clap that won't let go.
> Index fingers kiss the chin.

Instinctive greeting
followed by *Chumreapsur*,
yielding at hello.

Sompeah
> is when fingertips
> encounter a chin
> chanting Pali in monotone
> legs folded parallel,
> respectfully tucked.

Monks in golden robes
preserve Buddha's teachings.
Attendees surrender themselves
in the makeshift Bronx temple.

Nose of an AK-47
grazes a daughter's bangs
her bent knees smothered in soil,
her posture, a defeated slump.

Sompeah
> is when palms lock
> against the chin,
> sobs choked by bullets.

Music Doesn't Put Food On the Table

You eat now, why you sing?

There a time for eat
and time for sing.

Now—it time for eat.

Trespass

Our languages are broken.
These new tongues,
still on loan,
are fractured
in a language of pain.

Natives hum of trespass
among their borders
in a swelling moan.

These American shores
experience waves
of amassed culture.

Every English word
is a betrayal of our past.

Mother Monologue #1

You want Chinese bun? I buy it. This your favorite. Why you eat like that? That not nice. Oh—now you eat like high-class with knife and fork. You know, your Daddy he bad to me. He not nice when he young. He leave me home with you two and the baby then go spend the money, gamble the whole paycheck.

I so scare. Your Daddy give me $10. I lock you guy in the house. I tell Sothy not open the door to nobody. Then I run in the supermarket and buy the food on sale. All the chip. All the cookie.

Your poor brother alway hungry. He the one I love the most. In Pol Pot time, I gave him all my rice but not good enough. Now I buy you guy any food you want.

Initiation

In the photo, the child is covered
in red from calf to shoulder
facing the mountains.
Smoke brushes across its peaks.

The border of the refugee camp
parallels her horizon.
She stands on the edge,
a short wall among
a landscape of taupe ruin.
She relives the memory
of the soldier.

First he prays,
                    then thrusts,
draws out
                    her blood.
He prays again.

Day after day
            he grunts,
loads,
            imprints himself
on her history.

Back to the camera,
her red shirt is a bloodstain
on youth,
her hands
pressed against her backside
re-enacting
the first memory of bondage.

This Your Mother Say (or Mother Monologue #2)

Make sure   you marry.
Make sure   you marry a man.
Make sure   you marry who you love.
Make sure   a man love you.

Make sure you marry
        a man
        who love you
        more than
        you love him.

Mother's Call

Alo?

Chumpreapsur, Sister.
        You eat yet?
            Good. Good.

I want tell you

      PLEASE

      tell your son
            stop touch my daughter!

      Ueuy

You watch out
    or

      I drop-kick him till he wanna die!   Understand!?!

Bronx Childhood

Child, she says
this is what they look like.
From the bamboo fine-toothed comb
she pulls out a lice nit
then smashes it
between two thumbnails
like beef under her incisors.
Quietly she continues
through the black mop
of her daughter's hair
in the apartment
where the landlord
doesn't install bug screens.

In summers
the children slept
with windows open
awoke to mysterious insects
flown in from
the urban rock formation
they mistakenly
called a mountain.

The Fresh Oriental

Damn girl, why you ain't stomping roaches?
You so light when you jump Double Dutch.

Turn 'round, lemme braid your good hair.

Those pants you wearing are tight—
you gon' see your boyfriend today?

Heard that new Mariah Carey?
You sing it *good*, like a black girl.

You see Lisette looking in her mirror?
Ain't no makeup in the world
gonna make her look less ugly.

Miss your period?
My sister said drink hot Malta,
and you'll lose the baby.

He called you an "oriental bitch?"
Damn Bobby Brown-wannabe
with his Gumby-ass haircut.

His last name Bacon?
I eat him for lunch.

No Radio

i.
Sinn Sisamouth, Khmer poster boy
resonating tenor of every residence
off rooftops   on radios
a voice that chilled and warmed

Beloved, iconic face
decapitated   pasted over bodies in posters

ii.
My father is lost at Gun Hill Road in the Bronx.
A voice interrupts my daze
sprays 60's surf rock from the dashboard,
a Cambodian riding the radio waves.

Honey, this was the most famous singer in Cambodia.

iii.
Post-exodus Cambodia, 1975
two soldiers looked over the singer,
his palms pressed together in greeting.

He is asked to sing something
but muzzled by rattling AK-47s
echoing across hills. Children are playing soldier.
Fetuses ripped from wombs dangle
in nearby trees.

Yet when he opened his mouth
a flood of love melodies poured out.

iv.
An online friend revived
Bopha Reach Sroh
over a hip-hop instrumental.

No one knows what happened to him.
It's said that the Khmer Rouge made him sing
before they shot him.

v.
The stench of the unburied
transmits across towers of bones.

Hold Your Peace, I Speak Now

We exchange chokeholds instead of rings.

It takes two 40 ounces to confess your love
only to sleep with your deafening snore.

Commitment is making it through airport security
with crystal meth rocks in your crotch.

The only white I wear is spilled dust
from your mirrors and money straws.

Your legs dangle from a second-story window
laughing at tequila-induced enemies.

You think girls *deserve* rape.

Attach names biologically wed to me:
slut—whore—baby

Threats of your hetero language—
I was gonna marry you.

Through another's hands
the veil is removed from my face.

Tutoring in Session

Miss—

I had my hands on the window
I legit
was gonna throw myself
out the window

              I think
I might have depression my mom
        asked me these questions
        when I answered them
             she said
Oh you get it from me
she got the medicine that start with a "z"
said she could split the,
what you call it you know
how much medicine you take?
yeah dosage
me and her is gonna share it

Miss--
you're the only one
who listens to me
even my guidance counselor don't
everybody--the teachers my mom
wants something
for me
I just wanna sleep

WHY they won't let me
                sleep?

Postcard from the Bronx Zoo

The Bronx bound two train intersects
forming a cross with Boston Road East Tremont.

Below train tracks, cultures exchange over fists
in a Muslim-owned convenience store.

Greasy egg rolls linger, saturate housing projects.
People live in boxes stacked into the sky.

An *iglesia* cross peaks the apartment landscape.

Confused tourists push strollers, carrying lives in backpacks
follow smartly-designed city signs toward the Bronx Zoo.

The morning donut truck is the only place
where coffee is still fifty cents.

Nubian goddesses with doorknocker earrings on cellphones
cross traffic, some toting children, past appreciative eyes.

Bachata and merengue blare
at Latin expats eating neon-shaved ices.

A car door slams somewhere, letting out
a looped medley of sirens and whistles waiting to be disarmed.

Evasion

The uptown number two train syncopates
in limping metallic claps.
Numerous eyes become
dark magnetic beads following me.
I struggle with my merchandise,
balancing a bag of toys
and battery-stuffed fanny pack.
I attached it on too tight.
The creases stay with me.
"One dollar!" I shout. "One dollar!" again.
I always hope to find similar eyes.
This stranger halts me:
"you got triple A?" batteries
to play their discman, walkman, radio,
video game or some other damn thing.
Young mothers with children coo at toys;
flashing yo-yos, whistles, bubblegum,
beepers filled with gum,
and assorted human-shaped brightly-colored plastic bubble blowers.
Then smack of big hands on small hands.
Moms shake their heads.
My name was "hey," "you" and "ex-CUSE me."
I nicknamed customers "one dollar," "thanks," too.
You can spot me at Grand Concourse, Harlem
and other uptown stops. My yellow skin reveals
ignorance from up- and downtown.
We sit at 96th street speaking loud
in Cantonese. With each arriving train,
a girl disappears.
Asians spot each other's signature cursive eyes.
I try to decipher them; I'm tempted to speak Chinese.
A girl is reading in the corner.
I smile; she pretends not to see me.
My cheeks turn pomegranate red.
In another world we would have been
friends or neighbors, in continent or street.
I walk by and slide the door behind me.
A final click tells me
I've left all those eyes behind.

Diction

My voice teacher
wants me to sing "pure" vowels
so I imagine a choir of virgins
singing *oh* and *ah*.

Mispronounced consonants
crush and crunch
in a betrayal of sounds.

Trills from the tongue are inevitable
in their sexual flutter.

In my memory,
I taste again my first French kiss,
his tongue lapping my salty neck
beside the swishing sea.

When I sing in French
he tells me to aspirate less,
conjuring images
of my first lesson
in shared exhalation and utterances.

Seeing Red

From your bed I thought
we caused the blackout.

I hold onto breath
as our tongues play,
our hands looking for places to land.

These small fingers are hungry,
body parts itchy,
skin wet from misty nights.
We fell asleep to the glow
of your computer monitor
across the room.

In the studio,
I sing lyrics about you.
The red light
wants to record
the best part of me.

From late-night Joe's pizza
to a standstill on a Soho sidewalk
subway map engraved
on the ground beneath us,
I wonder about stops.

Red signs
signal for locking up.

Ron Carter playing "Autumn Leaves"
fills your studio.
You joke about the benefits
of dating a bass player.

These songs remain.

***

                    Less than five seconds into
                  the ascending piano
            I know where I've landed in my memory.

        Every little thing she does is magic.
        Everything she does just turns me on.

You can't offer more than coffee,
songs, and that electric red hair.

***

Like Kimiko,
sometimes I forget I'm writing a poem.

***

I want to cast you off
as a convenient summer haircut.
One moment
you're embedded in my skin
the next, in strands on the cutting room floor.

Now you're Chinatown
Alphabet City, the West Village
Carlsberg, pizza crust,
Denmark, Scotland,
Radiohead, Chris Cornell,
The Police.

I was nearly everything to you
in those CDs
you customized for me
            now covered in scratches,
            barely playable.

Progression

We hear sadness in
descending melodies of jazz ladies.

Ella   Nina   Sarah   Dinah
     Billie   Aretha   Carmen

We are intervals,
the distance between two notes.
Minor is closer to you;
major is further.
Is this why I listen to sad songs?

Enharmonic means
two different spellings
for the same note.

Listen—
        I want to make chords with you
             in the right key.

Common Ground

Dragonflies welcome me
      past rice trails,
      past cows with ribs
            fading into vision
                  through gauze-like skin.

Takeo is author to father's childhood
home to singing ghosts
      and scorpions propelled from closets.

Countryside folk invite you home,
invite you to the fields: will you come to the *srai*?

Around slivers of bike paths, thin barriers between rice plots,
I stop before an ornate rectangular plot.

Family is planted here like rice. My grandparents interrupt the stalks.

A poke of incense introduces me.
           My uncle chants in Khmer:

> *Your grandchild has come,*
> *all the way from America!*
> *And how beautiful, look at her!*
> *She's even as tall as you!*

I throw my head back in laughter. He replies:

> *Ah, she can understand,*
> *but she cannot speak back.*

We had the latter in common.

Baptism

My brother is lost in Cambodia.
I search the Killing Caves of Phnom Sampeau
where childish scrawl entreat donations,
a scratch resembling blood,
redemption for purchase.

Above Sampeau
reminders are skulls, already cliché
in the country of death paddies.
In this city on the hill
novice monks
                dream on the ground
                        draped in their robes
on limestone floors   a canvas of red and orange.
Thirty years ago
crimson bled   into igneous rust.

Jostled off cliffs,
        countrymen
              wait in agony
                future corpses
                   stacked
                     on the jagged hill.

***

Darkness is abundant.
I was their comrade one morning and now
surrounded by phantom flesh; the smell tingles.
You cannot imagine the loneliness—
        where is my rebirth
        to save me from this hell?

In the land of enlightenment, the stones cry out.

Voices inundate my path
      to the fountain,
sprawled on the hillside,
      hidden in the catacombs.
This is a country full of wraiths.

***

Chopsticks and noodle strands
mark the morning meal.
Will I remember you
for the pork broth
or my parents
beneath the temple's archway
in my viewfinder?
Mango tree leaves flutter
beside the shack
where you dispersed   in the wind.

You are embedded in me
as palm trees at sunset
      in Battambang,
a cousin's awkward English,
my incomplete Khmer,
or the first argument
where mother remains angry.
I slept with geckos
the night the terrain absolved us.

Above Phnom Sampeau,
    monks rained
    holy water
    above my head,
delicate kiss of orange blossom petals.

Mekong Song

I compose you letters in the air
among scattered saffron dust on this road.

Darling pineapples with golden flesh
call for attention in roadside display.

Vendors in conical straw hats heckle motorists
in facemasks, who reply with shrill retorts.

Time slows down to the soft folds
of a monk's crimson robe in traffic.

The day departs in turmeric hues
across the Phnom Penh sky.

A two-stringed fiddle announces
a resplendent wedding of silk and sashes.

Pulls of the bow resonate across
my ribcage and continents to you.

I am the longing in its timbre,
the ache in the string's tension.

Monsoon Monk

He wrings out the day
from the wet red robe
parts dangling
fabric folding against crevices,
sweat stains in tropical summer
this shoeless novice
saturated by the monsoon
during daily alms.

Circumference

The women don robes of bone
heads carved in moon cycles.

Their staggered sandal-shuffle kicks
road into dust, ordained steps,
spokes on the dharma wheel.

One compares her body to a wound
as she wraps cloth around herself.

One courtesan is released
from obligation of her various lips
and men seeking to fill it.

The wife who bore
crowns of children
circles a shrine clockwise.

Of cyclical desires extinguished
one nun writes,
I am quenched.

Reincarnation

I came of age
in the arms of Lord Shiva.
He welcomes with stone,
sculpted arms.
I slurp curry, crimson
as a monk's robe
tinged with the sun
on his morning alms,
what locals call "pig's blood."

I think of you
as the wind in Battambang.
I hear mother's murmur
as she searches for her past
on the stranger's land.
What remains of you is gone.
Sandals kick the dirt
into a hiss of spray.

That cold night you died
boughs of palm trees shuddered.

***

A smokescreen of incense covers our relatives.
Palms clutch apologies
chant in Pali before your name,
inscribed on offerings.

We are a family of alliterations,
shared consonants echo
generations in every utterance.

Sothear, Sothy, Srou, Sri, Srau, Sreng,
Sarah, Soriya, Han, Haun,
Phai, Phoun, Phoum, Pho, Pheng
Sokunthary, Sokuntharith

Beneath the Ground

A prayer summons me back.

Sutras revive
generations who return
with folded hands and whispers,
a prod of incense.

The earth is snug.
Incense burns to ash.

The monks you requested
murmur in monotone
naked as their shaved scalp.

I lie beside the rice stalks,
as if only to smell incense
from beneath the ground,
awaiting harvest
and rebirth.

Something Borrowed

I don't understand these natives
who wear my features.

I have no names
for countless cousins
only adjectives:
older or younger; brother or sister.
I fumble with borrowed language
of my childhood memories,
conjure images of my brothers.

Khmer language makes
relatives of strangers
creates blood mixed with mine.

I am transplant with transfusion.

Mornings in Phnom Penh
rouse to nuptial gongs
amid this hotel complex.
The employee knew
my gold hoop earrings and breakfast.
Still unraveling this tongue,
I misspoke her for a dear sister.

At the front desk
my engagement ring glows
before her fresh face.
She giggles with excitement.

Molding

Cambodian girls
in roadside salons
idolize them in curls.

Eternal female
sculpted for worship,
protector of the temple city.

Communist bullets
graze stone nipples.

Humanized by the King,
royal court dancers are poised
in gleaming headdress.

In twilight
an apsara
costume slumped
beside the royal bed.

Storytelling hands and feet
ancestral mudras,
reminiscent of lotus
unfurling beside the Buddha.

Foreigners cup their breasts
shiny from years of exploration,
hold them captive
in their viewfinder
to retrieve for pleasure
in future moments.

Dear Grandmother,

We peaked at Angkor Wat,
saw the red sandstone of Bantei Srei,
the citadel of women.
Ornate arches curved
into thighs and hips of women:
homage to the devata,
a fortress of deities.

My last day in Phnom Penh
you made eggs; my beloved staple
tastes impossibly delicious
beside somlau machou,
this country's chicken soup.
I let myself miss you.

Baguettes are sold by men on cyclos
in baskets strapped to their backs.
I imagine bread dough
beaten as it rises.
I try not to need you.
I want to push it down.

The lines on your skin
map my lineage
like a family recipe.

It's easier not to see your face.
To know you is to feel you,
to love and lose you
when you leave me.

Pochentong Farewell in Khmer

Now that I've seen your face, I am going to miss it.

Embody

1.
Rain limits and frees; the sun-loving majority stays
while I relish ten-blocks beside dogwood trees.

2.
Indecipherable languages beckon like elaborate prayer rugs
with designs diverse as world tongues.

3.
A co-worker's fasting means lunch money in my palm;
I would trade sustenance for that kind of faith.

4.
In a dream, white shirt and tie interrogate about The Book of Revelations.
I answer, "My parents are Buddhists."

5.
In my new home, I want the bliss of Khmer bodhisattvas, saffron-hued and all,
chanting the ancient language beside my Bed, Bath & Beyond curtains.

6.
The doctor called you a cheese doodle at two months and 1.57 centimeters.
These 9 months are not a song about one's self.

Postpartum Depression on Loop

The nursery soon darkens with a lullaby
tinkling from a plastic butterfly projector.
A baby alienates her with a cry.
In one day, she became a protector.

Tinkling from a plastic butterfly projector,
she absorbs the music for future replays.
In one day she became a protector.
A lasting scar paired with pills leave her dazed.

She absorbs the music for future replays
through an iPod, a mix of wistful songs.
A lasting scar paired with pills leave her dazed
in this eternal day. The mother longs

through an iPod, a mix of wistful songs.
She returns from her daily walk to silence.
In this eternal day, the mother longs
for an end. This new world makes her tense.

She returns from her daily walk to silence.
A baby alienates her with a cry
for an end. This new world makes her tense.
The nursery soon darkens with a lullaby.

Morning Song

I can hear you calling
in a hunger cry
to reveal your need.

I can hear you coo
as you discover your hands
and your eyes light up.

As you soften your voice
I'll be the embrace you seek
to carry you to sleep.

I imagine you will rise
with the sun, my morning call
at the start of each new day.

Ode to Mother's Sarong

Refugee wallpaper
for family portraits
a knotted baby carrier
on mother's back
monsoon covering

black and blue
night tapestry
midnight inquiries
unwrapped questions
to be encased
covered
coveted

a heart-wrap
rice field shawl
Mekong towel
black hair threads
cross blue rivers
cover of ocean and kmao
between thighs

in jungle flight
this mother-landing
carried my brother
and monsoon rains
across infinite jungle

When Motherhood is Suffering

Mother. Mommy. Ma. Mai. Mak. Aba. Ima. Maman.

Start by saying her name. Call it. Cry it. Who else hears her cry? Husband gambled the rent, cheated with his family's help. Her money goes to people who don't respect her. The hotel guests silence her with tips or stinginess. Dirty rooms, like pigs, like savages. Bathrooms. The quiet shame of an older woman having an accident on the bed. She soothes her, hushes her, tells her "Don't worry, Mama. I clean up." The grateful eyes that follow her movements.

Mommy is tired.

"Mother, I'm cold," said Sothea, when he died in her arms at the age of 3. *I think about him everyday*. Trivialities that take up space to cover silence of pain. Opinion. Disappointment. Regret. She hides behind the façade of happiness. Who is she? Dismember. Re-member.

Daughter-in-Waiting

Mak,
I'm watching for your cues
to know
who is older
who is younger
more ancient
whose legs
I can't cross over
whose head
I must bow lower
when I walk past
who deserves more respect
who is a brother
who is an uncle
ancestor
royalty
teacher
wearing titles that hold
entire relationships
that determine
worlds of dynamics
shift rooms and expectations
how much to widen the circle
how robust.

I'm waiting,
Mak,
for you to tell me
if this woman
is your elder or junior
if I should see her
as my sister or aunt.

I'm watching as you respond
to different titles
from others.
But you are my mother.

So Mak,
tell me how to connect.

First Generation Cambodian American Mother Facebook Typo

"Good luck, homey."

"Good Luck, Homey"

You know,
          my life
                    good.
Now I know
like…I happy.
I use the skype,
          facebook
                    and I not alone.

I take the picture
put on the facebook
and EVERYBODY like it.
I not know how to read before
but now
                    I GOOD.

How you write "beautiful"?
I want to write when I see
the picture of my friend
say "how are you"

          "look good, sister"

That how you spell?
Oh my god. I never know.
Now I know.
I learn so much from you.

You see honey, you my good luck.

Good View for a No. 2

There is a bathroom window
so large in this cabin
the trees feel like a museum display.

The sink is clogged from extra hair
trimmed off a husband's beard.

The toothpaste tube is crimped
and squeezed for its last bits.

The garbage can is agape.

The child enjoys a good sitting
every night, sings while squatting,
wants to write a poem called
"Good View for a No. 2."

From the toilet seat you can see
a tree ready to fall.

So when the time comes for firewood,
there's only the sound of you
cutting off a log.

Mother Tongue

Cambodian script resembles
slurped noodles in Phnom Penh,
immersed in orange curry
peppers of blood red and turmeric,
golden as my cousin's monastic robe.

I wanted only noodle dinners
for two weeks as a child.
Mother sliced strips of beef
like em dashes.
They stiffened
in the heat of her broth.

Some characters resemble
the outline of my daughter's pinky,
sometimes inverted
a loop beneath or above.

Every morning I detangle the knots
she creates with her dreams,
draw a line to part her hair.
Once combed,
I braid her hair into sense
just as I unravel
the curls of this script
trace family lines
pronounced on my hip,
curved in my eyes,
looped like my mother's sarong
coming undone.

Reading Between the Ribcage

Late summer and glowing street lamps
trace lines in my vision,
a heady Parisian scene as I pass.

In the sanctuary
of Église Saint-Éphrem
Bach cello suites echo in the dark cavity.
The bow sweeps up the church beams
and scrapes down its foundation.

In the front pew a woman rests
her head against a man.
He rubs her palm,
keeping the pulse.

God and the cosmos
are in Bach's arpeggios,
vibrations of the universe
in spelled-out chords,
double stops,
an arm stretched across
a cello's bridge
in a yawn.

With each pull of the bow,
music enters our ribcage
and notes fall
in between our bones.

The Estate

A broken Mezuzah at the entrance
with its inside missing
cancels the word of her god.

Spots of green mold
splatter the roof.

Midwinter, heat escapes
through hidden gaps.

The growing mice problem
one can only hear.

Years of dog hair
discovered in the closet.

The den of black and white photos
are a shrine to her youth.

In her final days of cancer
the bedroom is free of curtains,
to allow every miraculous sunrise.

This Is Your Inheritance
for Soriya

I see years of history before you,
my Cambodian daughter.

I named you in Sanskrit
as the sun, a Hindu god.

You contain the darkness of our genocide.

You are the potential of our refugees,
to come back from near extinction.

I see you
in a stone homage to gods and kings
among the Bayon's tower of echoing faces.

You are the *Danseuses Cambodgiennes*
who wooed Rodin to that Paris dock,
immortalized in watercolor.

You will be too much
or not enough.

They will mispronounce you, misspell you.
Yogis will hear your name and think sun salutations.

Remember, those who bow to your light
must not burn from your sun.

Pulse in 2

You are my breath mark.

,

I try to steady
the metronome
in my heart.

Don't Let Your Heritage Be Past Tense

Think of your great-grandmother
in woven silk,
countless threads through her hands
weaving lines   intersecting
her face and palms,
her children who compose
your motherland fabric.

Songsters of Cambodia's golden age—
Ros SreySothea, Sin Sisamouth, Penn Ran—
blare from past decades in static
singing across time
through a rusty accordion.

We have numerous words for eat:
see, nyam, hoap, chan, pisaah.
Each bite is love.
Yiey asks if you are hungry—
because it took thirty years
to say *I love you* like an American.

You imagine a future not yet past
of grandfather's garden in Georgia,
untended in the southern red clay
where fruit trees have taken root.
Someday you will taste dragonfruit
on par with his on the streets of Phnom Penh.
Tha's face is bright when he sees you
enjoy its flesh, studded with seeds.

He says, *I wish I could be here
when the apple trees bloom.*

Thank You

Ms. Tepp, Mr. Lugano, my dearest Josh Wilner, Andres Andrade, Kimiko Hahn, Marilyn Hacker, Yerra Sugarman, Eric Chernov, Aracelis Girmay, Natalie Diaz, Barbara Gleason, Missy Watson, Tom Peele.

Bryan Thao Worra, Peuo Tuy, Bunkong Tuon, Lin Da Saphan, Dave Liao, Linda Thach, Chakriya Un, Chhaya Choum at Mekong NYC, Silong Chhun, Chenda Bao, Moniphal Bing, Laura Ly, Yeng Chheangly, Phina So, Khaty Xiong, Abigail Licad, Catzie Vilayphonh, Lao community, Cambodian Living Arts, CALAA board of directors. Tim Frederick, Jackie Sherbow, Stephanie Davis, Heather Talty, Joe Okonkwo, Malcolm Chang, Allison Escoto, Aida Zilelian-Silak.

"Milk" crew: Allison, Ananda, Ben, Claire, Andrea, Cynthia, Taylor, Tyler, JP, Erin, and Asa-cake. Patty Tumang, Jinky de Rivera, Monica Sok, Sarah Key, Rachelle Parker, Marina Blitshteyn, Cathy Linh Che, Jason Erik Lundberg, Holly Lee Warren, George and Joan Kovach, Olivia Kate Cerrone, Catherine Parnell, Giedra Kregzdys, Jyothi Natarajan, Emily Yoon, Sophia Hussein, Ashley Strosnider, Wendy Chin-Tanner, Maria Lisella, JCAL, Hyphen, Lauren Clark, Poets House, Tillman Miller. FH Station House: Nick, Steve, Steve-O, Bobby, Jordan, Kris, Jeremy, Victor, Vito, Paolo, Pascale, Miles, Gabe, Stig, Bryce, Barry, Debo, Kyle, Chris, Dave, Tslil, Araina, Jayne, Adam, Glenn, Lance. QL: Meera Nair, Jared Harel, Mary Lannon, Nancy Agabian, Catherine Fletcher, Dominick Gregory, Crystal Yeung, Kevin Kudic, Jesse Rice-Evans, Allia Matta, William Lung, Maria Vint, Helen Dano, Zubair Hack, Jin-Xiang Yu, Liliya Ugay, David Schober, Lee Ryder, qt Jeff "Redboy" Graham, Mary Giaimo, Lisa Smith, Scott Corr, Pia Inthavong-Chow, Diane Allford, Alan Trotman, and Chanel Matsunami Govreau.

Heather Buchanan and Randall Horton.

Mommy and Daddy, Sokuntharith/Jammy, Sothy, Ellen Sea, Takeo and Phnom Penh family, Jacki and Greg Potter, Cyd Potter, Emily Siy. My daughter, Soriya Annabel, for her unconditional love, forgiveness, unending curiosity and creativity. And to my partner in all aspects of my life, Jacob Gregory Potter, there is no me without you.

About the Author

Sokunthary Svay is a Pushcart-nominated Khmer writer and musician from the Bronx, New York. She and her family were refugees from Cambodia who survived the genocidal Khmer Rouge regime. She is the poetry editor for *Newtown Literary*. A founding member and Board President of the Cambodian American Literary Arts Association (CALAA), her work has been published internationally in Malaysia, London and Phnom Penh. Svay was a subject in *New York Magazine*'s "Living in a Sanctuary City" and featured in the New York Immigration Coalition's *This is Our NY*, broadcast in Times Square. Additional credits include *Homelands: Women's Journeys Across Race, Place and Time, LONTAR: Journal for Southeast Asian Speculative Fiction, Mekong Review, Perigree* and *The Margins*. She is a past Willow Arts Alliance Fellow and recipient of the First Friday Residency at the Jamaica Center for Arts and Learning, and the 2017-2019 American Opera Projects' Composer & the Voice Fellow.

CPSIA information can be obtained
at www.ICGtesting.com
Printed in the USA
BVHW072020120821
614310BV00002B/11